BY THE SAME AUTHOR

Discovering What Garter Snakes Do
Life in the Dark
The Optical Illusion Book
Pets in a Jar
The Rockhound's Book
Science Projects in Pollution

by Seymour Simon

illustrated by Susan Bonners

what do you want to know about guppies?

what do you want to know about guppies?

Four Winds Press   New York

Library of Congress Cataloging in Publication Data

Simon, Seymour.
  What do you want to know about guppies?

  Bibliography: p.
  Includes index.
  SUMMARY: Discusses the guppy's history,
setting up an aquarium, caring for and breeding
guppies, dealing with their diseases, and choosing
tank mates for them.
  1. Guppies—Juvenile literature. [1. Guppies]
I. Bonners, Susan. II. Title.
SF458.G8S55   639'.375'3   77–5930
ISBN 0–590–07412–1

Published by Four Winds Press
A Division of Scholastic Magazines, Inc., New York, N.Y.
Text copyright © 1977 by Seymour Simon
Illustrations copyright © 1977 by Scholastic Magazines, Inc.
Printed in the United States of America
Library of Congress Catalog Card Number: 77–5930
2 3 4 5   81 80 79 78

For Joyce

and our first guppies,
Hansel and Gretel

contents

what do you
      want to know
         about
            guppies?

1.

the curious history of the guppy

Guppies are small, tropical freshwater fish. In the wild, they are not much to look at. The female guppy is a drab grayish-green color. Each scale on its body is edged with a dark line. A mature female is about one and one-half inches long.

A male guppy is slightly shorter than a female and has a slimmer body. Male guppies are more brightly colored than females. Mixtures of reds, blues, greens, and violets cover the back parts of their bodies. At one time, a popular nickname for guppies was "rainbow fish."

In nature, guppies eat small water animals including large numbers of mosquito "wrigglers." Because of their help in keeping down the numbers of mosquitos, guppies were imported often into tropical countries around the world. Nowadays wild guppies are found all over the tropics. In fact, it is difficult to find out whether guppies are native to countries such as Mexico, or whether they were imported and became wild years ago.

Guppies usually live in the warm waters of low-lying ponds, lakes, and slow moving streams. But they also can live in the colder waters of higher elevation streams and in partly salty waters close to seashores.

Water temperature in these different spots varies from 65° Fahrenheit (18° Celsius) to higher than 80° Fahrenheit (27° Celsius). Some guppies live in waters that contain large amounts of dissolved minerals. Others live in places where the water only has small traces of dissolved minerals.

The guppy is so adaptable to different water conditions that it can survive even the salt content in ocean water. Of course, a guppy just can't be dumped from fresh water into salt water. The change must be made slowly, over a period of several days. But after a guppy adapts to its new water surroundings, it seems to be able to live without difficulty.

Female guppies seem to be hardier than males. In experiments in which temperature and other water conditions are changed rapidly, more males than females usually die. Guppy owners sometimes observe the same thing happening in their aquariums. If a water heater accidentally fails, the males often die in large numbers, while most of the females seem to survive.

The greater hardiness of the female may partly account for the curious fact that many more adult females than adult males are found in nature. In the wild, the guppy is preyed upon by other animals including larger fishes such as the blue acara and the pike cichild. The colorful males are easier to see than the drab females and may make a better target for some predators.

Guppies have been kept in aquariums in homes for many years. A German scientist, Wilhelm Peters, first collected guppies in Venezuela in 1859. Two years later, another scientist found guppies on the Caribbean island of Barbados.

The popular name of the fish, "guppy," came from the name of the third scientist who collected them, Dr. Robert John Lechmere Guppy.

Female

Male

Male

Guppies in the wild.

Dr. Guppy found some small fish on the island of Trinidad, off the northern coast of South America. In 1866, he sent specimens of the fish back to the British Museum. There the fish were thought to be a newly discovered species. They were given the scientific name, *Girandinus guppyi,* in honor of their supposed discoverer.

But as it turned out, the fish from Venezuela, Barbados, and Trinidad all belonged to the same species. So the correct scientific name should have been an earlier one that Peters gave to the fish. To avoid all this name confusion, scientists finally gave a new name to the fish, *Lebistes reticulatus.* It made little difference. Everyone keeps calling the fish a guppy.

Veiltail guppies (both male). Type bred by Paul Hahnel.

In 1908 and 1909, a collection of live guppies was sent to some aquarium keepers in Germany. In 1911, the guppy made its first appearance in the United States. In a short time, the guppies were bred and their offspring distributed to fish fanciers in different parts of the country.

Guppies became very popular as aquarium fish in the mid-thirties, when brightly colored and large-sized strains were developed. In the fifties, Paul Hahnel, of New York City, developed a fancy guppy strain with a large veiltail. They were immensely popular. Soon, guppy breeders all over the country developed their own strains. Many had distinctive colors and differently shaped fins.

Nowadays you can find a wide variety of guppy strains in the aquariums of pet stores. Veiltails, swordtails, delta tails, golds, reds, blacks, even the original wild types can be found. Prices range from just a few pennies for the wild strain of guppies (one store recently advertised 100 guppies for $3.98), to $5 or $10 apiece for some of the fancier kinds.

Guppies remain one of the most popular of all aquarium fishes. They are hardy, demand little room, and are easily fed and kept in almost any kind of container. Because guppies give birth to living young, even beginners can breed and raise them at home.

Yet guppies still present a challenge to advanced hobbyists. New strains of different colors and sizes are continually being developed. Every time you visit a tropical fish dealer, there seems to be a new guppy variety in the tanks. The small fish with the funny name has become one of the most widely kept pets in the world.

⋈ ⋈ ⋈ ⋈ ⋈ ⋈ ⋈ ⋈ ⋈ ⋈ ⋈ ⋈ ⋈ ⋈ ⋈ ⋈ ⋈ ⋈

2.
setting up
a guppy aquarium

Of all the tropical fishes that are seen in aquariums, guppies are one of the easiest to maintain. Guppies can live in large aquarium tanks or in small fishbowls. You can even keep guppies in wide-mouthed glass jars that were originally used for pickles or mayonnaise.

Three or four guppies per gallon of water is a safe number to keep in a regular aquarium tank. For example, a 5-gallon tank that measures 14 inches long by 8 inches wide provides plenty of room for 20 guppies. The surface area of the water is more important than the depth of the water. Each guppy needs about 5 square inches of surface area to survive and do well in an aquarium.

Because of their small surface areas, jars or fishbowls with a narrow neck are a poor choice for an aquarium. If you must use a container with a narrow neck, fill it to its widest point. A low-standing, wide fishbowl is a better choice than a deeper, narrow fishbowl.

To find the surface area of a round container, measure across at the water level. Take half of this number and multiply it by itself. Multiply the result by $3\frac{1}{7}$. For example, suppose your fishbowl is 6 inches across at the water level. Half of that is 3 inches. Multiplying 3 by itself, you get 9. Multiplying 9 by $3\frac{1}{7}$, you get a little over 28 square inches. That would be enough room for 5 guppies.

Before you place guppies in an aquarium, you must prepare it. Clean the aquarium with water but do not use any soap or detergent. Even a slight trace of soap remaining in the aquarium will kill the guppies. If there are any dirty spots on the glass that you want to remove, scrub them with a handful of coarse salt or with a soap-free cleaning brush. Rinse the tank with running water when you are finished.

Set your aquarium in a permanent spot in your room before you fill it. Water is very heavy. It weighs over eight pounds per gallon. A five-gallon aquarium when filled with water and gravel can easily weigh fifty pounds or more. It's easier to carry water to fill an empty aquarium than to carry a water-filled aquarium around a room.

Run the tap water in your sink for several minutes. This will help get rid of any minerals that might have been picked up in the plumbing. Use a plastic bucket to fill your aquarium three fourths full of water.

Ambulia

Vallisneria

Hygrophila

Let the water stand undisturbed for a day or two until it clears and the bubbles are gone. You can keep guppies in a bare tank filled with water only, but plants make the aquarium look more natural and are good for the fish, too. Green plants take in waste products such as carbon dioxide that guppies give off. The plants use these wastes to produce food for themselves. Along with the food they make, plants also give off oxygen which animals need to breathe.

Plants in an aquarium also provide hiding places for baby guppies. Without places to hide from the larger fishes in an aquarium, most baby guppies will be eaten before they have a chance to mature. In nature, this is not altogether a bad thing. If most babies weren't eaten, the numbers of guppies would soon become so great that many would die of lack of food and overcrowded conditions.

Most pet stores that carry guppies also sell aquarium plants. There are many different kinds of plants that should do well in a home aquarium. Vallisneria, Sagittaria, sword plants, Cabomba, Nitella, Ambulia, and Hygrophila are good choices. Ask the aquarium dealer for his suggestions. Healthy plants look crisp and not wilted or soft.

Some aquarium plants can live just by floating in water. But most aquarium plants will do better if they are rooted in gravel. Do not use beach sand or any other fine grain sand in an aquarium. Fine sand grains clump together and do not allow the roots of plants to grow. A coarse grade of natural gravel or a colored gravel is best for an aquarium.

Sagittaria

Cabomba

Amazon Swordplant

Nitella

Use a clean plastic pail to rinse out the gravel thoroughly in running water. Spread out the cleaned gravel at the bottom of your aquarium to a depth of two or three inches. Smooth it out so that the surface of the gravel slopes gently down to the front of the tank. This looks better and also allows decaying leaves and waste materials to pile up in one spot so that they can be removed easily.

Use your fingers to make a hole in the gravel for a plant's roots. Spread out the roots in the hole and cover them with gravel. The gravel should cover only the roots, not the leaves of the plant. Plants without roots and those with short roots can be allowed to float freely in the water.

In order for the plants to get enough light, you either need a bulb in a reflector above the aquarium, or a spot near a sunny window. An hour or two of direct sunlight is enough for most plants in an aquarium. The advantage of a bulb in a reflector is that you can regulate the amount of light that the plants get. You also can view your guppies in the evening or whenever else you would like.

You can purchase a reflector for either fluorescent or incandescent bulbs. Fluorescents are more expensive to start with but use less electricity and may be cheaper in the long run. A warm light fluorescent is better for the plants than a cool white color. Incandescent bulbs also can be purchased in many colors. Leave an incandescent on for about eight to ten hours each day. A fluorescent can be left on a few hours longer.

Any light, natural or artificial, is perfectly all right as long as the aquarium gets enough of it. Too little light will leave the plants spindly and weak. But too much light will turn the water green and it will be difficult to see through.

The green water is caused by microscopic plants called algae. Algae multiply quickly under bright light. Some algae growing on the back or sides of the tank is fine. It helps the guppies in the same ways as do the other green plants growing in an aquarium. But too much algae floating in the water not only makes the guppies difficult to see but also may become dangerous for the fish. If the amount of light changes, large amounts of algae may die and decay. Decaying algae can turn your aquarium into a smelly mess.

If you get too much algae growing in your aquarium, reduce the number of hours you keep the electric light on each day. If you are using sunlight only, you can cut down the amount of light reaching the aquarium in this way. Tape several thicknesses of tissue paper to the side of the aquarium exposed to the sunlight. By varying the number of layers you can adjust the amount of sunlight reaching the water.

The best temperature for your guppies is about 75° Fahrenheit (24° Celsius). But guppies can adapt to somewhat cooler or warmer temperatures as long as the adjustment is slow. If your room temperature is kept above 65° Fahrenheit (18° Celsius) during cooler weather, you probably don't need a special heater for your aquarium. You can purchase an inexpensive aquarium thermometer to check on the water temperature.

Reflector and light

Tissue taped to back to screen sun.

Gravel piled up toward back

But if your room temperature drops down low during the night, then you should consider buying an aquarium heater. An aquarium heater is hung from the back of the aquarium into the water. A line cord from the heater is plugged into an electric outlet. A dial on top of the heater can regulate the temperature at which it will keep the water. Heaters are rated by the amount of watts of electricity they use. To find the correct wattage, multiply the number of gallons of water by five. For example, a five-gallon aquarium should use a twenty-five-watt heater.

Other accessories that will help you maintain your guppies in good shape are a net and a dip tube. A net will help you catch and remove guppies from one tank to another. A dip tube will clean up dirt and other materials from the gravel. Both are quite inexpensive and can be purchased from any pet store that carries tropical fishes.

Air pumps and filters are more expensive aquarium helpers. A filter will clean the water in an aquarium continuously day and night. An air pump is used to power the filter. Air pumps also bubble air through the water. The constant movement of air will increase the numbers of guppies that can be safely kept in an aquarium.

Daphnia

Tubifex worms

Brine shrimp

⋈ ⋈ ⋈ ⋈ ⋈ ⋈ ⋈ ⋈ ⋈ ⋈ ⋈ ⋈ ⋈ ⋈ ⋈ ⋈ ⋈ ⋈ ⋈

3.

caring for your guppies

The best way to feed your guppies is to give them only a little food at a time, but do it often. If you give them too much food at once, the excess will decay and pollute the aquarium water. Overfeeding is probably the most common cause of pollution in a home aquarium.

A guppy's appetite is linked to its surroundings. Higher temperatures, longer periods of light, crowded conditions, the amount of plants, and other conditions will affect the way a guppy breathes and grows. The faster a guppy breathes and grows the more it will want to eat.

If you are using dry or flake food, feed only enough so that all of it can be eaten in five minutes. In this way you can feed guppies three to five times a day, morning, afternoon, and evening. If you can't manage so many feedings a day, feed them once in the morning and once in the evening.

This girl is feeding live Daphnia to her fish.

There are many different kinds of prepared foods for guppies that you can buy. It is a good idea to vary the kinds of food that you give your guppies. Use a flake food as a basic item in their diet each day. Supplement this with a feeding of freeze-dried or frozen brine shrimp or some other freeze-dried or frozen food available in your pet store. Small, cut-up pieces of cooked shrimp or clams are also good for your guppies.

Live foods are good for guppies but not really necessary if the rest of their diet is a varied one. Daphnia are one of the live foods that are sometimes available in the spring months. This small relative of shrimp and lobster is also called a water flea. A cloud of daphnia in a pond looks like thousands of fleas hopping up and down in the water but getting no place. Daphnia are usually red in color though they may be green and also gray.

Daphnia can be fed to guppies by just putting a quantity of them in the aquarium. The guppies will eat as much as they want. The remaining daphnia will live in the water of the aquarium for a number of days and be available as food. Daphnia, like fishes, need oxygen, so too many of them placed in an aquarium at one time may cause discomfort to your guppies.

Still other live foods that may be available in pet stores include brine shrimp and tubifex worms. Brine shrimp are hatched and sold in salt water. For this reason they should be netted and placed in an aquarium, rather than poured into the water. Brine shrimp can live only for several hours in fresh water so don't feed too many of them to your guppies.

Tubifex worms live in waters that contain a good deal of mud and silt along with possible pollution. The worms should be washed thoroughly before being fed to your fish. The best way to do this is to place the worms in a plastic pail into which a slow, steady stream of cold water is flowing. Keep them this way for two or three hours. The living worms will bunch together at the bottom while the dead worms will be washed away.

Earthworms are generally much too large for guppies to eat. They can be used as food if you are willing to slice them up into small enough pieces so that they can be swallowed at one gulp. Wash the pieces before you drop them, one at a time into the aquarium. Make sure that the guppies eat each piece before you drop in the next.

Every other week you should clean out the collected sediment at the bottom of your aquarium. For this task, use a dip tube or a length of plastic hose as a siphon. A dip tube is placed over the sediment on the bottom. When you remove your thumb from the top of the tube, a small amount of water and sediment rush into the tube. The tube is then lifted out and overturned into a pail for disposal.

To use a plastic tube as a siphon, first fill it with water. Holding your fingers over each open end, hang one end of the tube over the side of the aquarium into a plastic pail. Hold the other end of the tube in the water near the sediment. Release your fingers. The water will rush out of the tube carrying sediment along with it.

Remove algae from the front glass with a cleaning pad of rough nylon or some other rough material that will not rust or break up in the water. Be sure that the pad is clean, free of any soap, and not used for anything else.

If you do not use an air pump or a filter, the water in your aquarium may be covered by a thin greasy-looking film. This can be removed easily by dragging a paper towel across the surface of the water from one end of the tank to the other. Repeat this several times until all traces of the film are gone. At the same time that you are cleaning the tank, check and clean the heater, the thermometer, and any other accessories that you are using.

Replace the water that you removed along with any water that has evaporated. Tap water usually contains a chemical called chlorine. Chlorine is added to drinking water to kill any harmful germs that may be present. But guppies may also be harmed by chlorine in their water. Allowing water to age for a day or two will remove any chlorine. Use a plastic or glass container to hold the water as it ages.

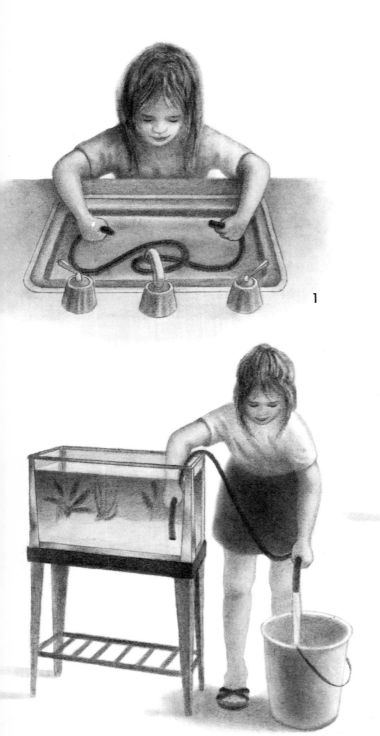

1

2

3

Guppies can safely swim from warmer to cooler spots in an aquarium. But changing a guppy from a tank of one temperature to another tank of a much different temperature should not be done. The guppy may start to shimmy or shake, or it may even go into shock and die. In the same way, water added to a guppy tank that contains water should be within two or three degrees of each other.

It is easier to catch a guppy with a large net than with a small net. Purchase a net that is at least three inches by four inches. When you net a guppy, try to trap it against a glass side of the aquarium. Tap on the glass so that the guppy swims deeper into the net. Raise the net quickly and place your free hand over the top to prevent the guppy from jumping out.

Place the net in the water into which you are transferring the guppy. Allow the guppy to swim out freely. Never dump a guppy into a tank from high above.

Most fish nets are made of nylon, which is a tough material. A guppy's fins and scales can easily be damaged by rough or frequent handling in a net. When you transfer a guppy from one tank to another, be as gentle as you can. The best way is not to handle a guppy at all unless you must.

Veiltail guppy (male)

Black Angelfish

◁▷ ◁▷ ◁▷ ◁▷ ◁▷ ◁▷ ◁▷ ◁▷ ◁▷ ◁▷ ◁▷ ◁▷ ◁▷ ◁▷ ◁▷ ◁▷ ◁▷ ◁▷

4.

guppies inside and outside

Look at a guppy swimming around in your aquarium. It spends most of the time near the surface of the water. A guppy feeds mostly at the surface and is attracted to any small floating object. Many of the features of a guppy's body are adapted to help it survive near the surface.

A guppy's head is sharply pointed. Its lower jaw curves upward to meet its smaller upper jaw. This helps it grab insects and other food animals that swim at the surface. In contrast, a bottom-feeding fish such as a catfish has a larger upper jaw that helps it pick up food from underneath.

A guppy has a low profile top fin. This fin, called a "dorsal," does not break the water's surface and leave a telltale wake behind. Imagine a long-finned angelfish swimming near the surface. Any predator could easily spot its trail and go after it.

Large eyes set on either side of its head help a guppy spot insects and also keep a lookout for danger. A large back (caudal) fin or tail gives a guppy a strong push for short bursts of speed needed to get to its prey or to avoid becoming prey itself.

Of course, a guppy can swim below the surface as well. It easily grabs food that is sinking and can also feed along the bottom. But in deeper aquariums or in nature, a guppy stays mostly near the surface.

Even though guppies have many color patterns, they are all darker colored near the top of their bodies and lighter colored underneath. This is called counter shading. When you look at guppies from above, their darker colors make them hard to spot against the ground and plants below. But when viewed from underneath, their lighter underparts blend in well with the lighter sky.

The different colors, dark-colored spots, and patches on a guppy's body help to break up its outline and make it more difficult to see. The better a guppy blends in with its surroundings, the less likely it is to be seen and eaten by a larger fish or some other predator.

At birth and up until about the fourth week, male and female guppies are about the same size and look much alike. The male has not yet developed its fancy colors and there are no differences as far as the eye can tell.

After the fifth week, the female grows larger than the male. A dark triangular area becomes visible at the back of the female's belly. This is called the gravid spot. All female guppies show this spot. When the young are born they pass through a vent at the back of the gravid spot.

The male begins to change, too. When it is about three-fourths of an inch long, it begins to develop an organ called a gonopodium. The gonopodium is a grooved tube through which droplets of sperm pass during mating. The gonopodium forms from the bottom back (anal) fin.

Both male and female guppies show a dark line along the length of

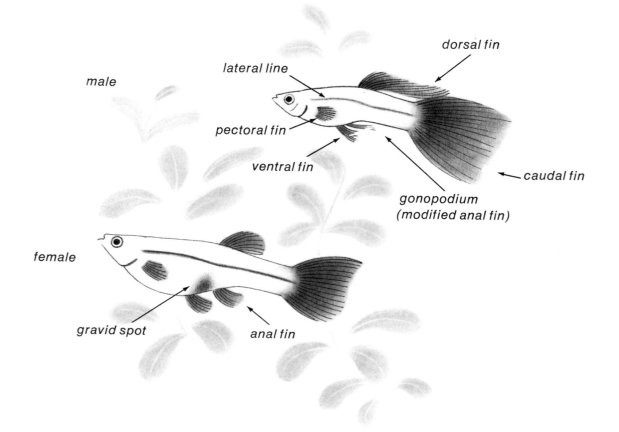

male

lateral line

dorsal fin

pectoral fin

ventral fin

caudal fin

gonopodium
(modified anal fin)

female

gravid spot

anal fin

their bodies. This is called a lateral line. The lateral line is made of very sensitive nerve endings. It helps a guppy sense the changing pressure of water on its body. A moving object in the water, a rock, or the sides of the aquarium reflect pressure waves in the water. Even in the dark, a guppy can swim about without hitting anything.

Watch how a guppy uses its fins to move around in the water. Its smaller fins are used like paddles to help the guppy balance. But when

swim bladder

it wants to move fast, the guppy bends its whole body and tail fin back and forth in short curves. A guppy can move surprisingly quickly. You'll see just how quickly a guppy can move when you try to catch one with a net.

Helping a guppy get around in the water is a structure within its body called a swim bladder or an air bladder. A guppy uses its swim bladder to remain at any level in the water. A little more air in the bladder and the guppy floats upward. A little less air in the bladder and the guppy sinks downward. The swim bladder keeps the guppy's weight very near the weight of an equal volume of water. This makes it easy for the guppy to get around with only a small push of its fins.

Like all other fishes, guppies need to breathe air to live. They do this by means of their gills. Watch how a guppy is constantly opening its mouth in the water. Water passes in through a guppy's mouth, through gill chambers on either side of its head, and then out through the gill flaps.

Dissolved oxygen in the water passes through thin skin in the gill chambers and into the guppy's bloodstream. At the same time, carbon dioxide, a waste gas made inside a guppy's body, passes out of the bloodstream into the water.

If there are too many fishes in an aquarium, the water becomes full of carbon dioxide. The fishes become uncomfortable and go to the surface to breathe. In such a crowded aquarium, you'll see the fishes gasping for air at the surface. The remedy is either to use a larger aquarium or to have fewer fishes.

Guppies can live for a time out of water as long as their gills and skin remain wet. You can use this fact to help you observe the way blood circulates in a guppy's body.

Here's how. Catch a guppy with a net and immediately wrap its body and head in some wet absorbent cotton. Make sure to handle the guppy gently. Place it on a glass slide. Put a few drops of water over its tail to keep it moist and then cover the tail with a glass cover slip. You should replace the guppy in its aquarium in no longer than five to ten minutes.

Place the slide under a microscope and observe the spread-out tail. You'll see what look like tiny dots moving through many blood vessels in the tail. The dots are really red blood cells. They carry oxygen through the guppy's body.

In some of the blood vessels, you'll see the blood moving quickly in spurts. These are arteries. They carry blood away from a guppy's heart. A guppy's heart has two chambers, called an auricle and a ventricle. Each time the heart pumps, blood spurts through the arteries. In other blood vessels, the blood moves more slowly and steadily. These are called veins. They carry blood back to the heart. The smallest blood vessels that you see are called capillaries. They make a kind of U-turn connecting the arteries to the veins.

Blood carries the materials that each of the cells in a guppy's body needs. Dissolved oxygen and carbon dioxide are carried by the blood. Wastes that are given off by the cells are carried by the blood. A guppy's body needs blood in much the same way that your body needs blood.

A guppy's skin is covered by tiny scales. As with larger fishes that you catch or see in the market, the scales cover the body in regular rows. One part of each scale grows from beneath the skin while the other end is free.

Just as the tiles protect a roof, a guppy's scales protect its body. The scales are hard and transparent. They are not as easily injured as soft skin. A guppy's color comes from cells in the skin beneath the scales. The color cells overlap one another to produce the many shades that make the rainbow colors of a guppy.

female

male

(highly magnified)

5.

from egg to adult

Young male guppies will court females when they are only six or seven weeks old, still a number of weeks from becoming mature. The courting ritual is a kind of back and forth dance in front of the female. During the dance the male guppy displays his tail and fins. Once in a while he takes a little nibble at the female's fins.

Often the female just seems annoyed at all this attention and tries to swim away. But the male is persistent. He follows the female all over the tank. In fact the only let up in his courtship behavior is during feeding time.

Finally there comes a time when the female is ready to mate. The male swims alongside the female. He swings his gonopodium forward and to the side. The tip of the gonopodium enters the female's vent and a large amount of sperm cells enters the female.

Some of the sperm cells unite with egg cells inside the female fertilizing them. Other sperm cells may be kept alive in the female for many months. These may be used to fertilize future sets of eggs that the female produces.

Older and larger females can carry several sets of eggs fertilized at different times. This helps to explain why females kept in an aquarium apart from males for many months can still give birth to young.

The eggs take about one month to develop in the female's body after they are fertilized. The length of time seems to be affected by water temperature and other conditions such as available food. Temperatures below about 68° F. (20° C.) seem to slow down development greatly. Temperatures above 80° F. (27° C.) speed up development.

The number of young that a female produces is variable. Young, small females sometimes produce only five or six newborn young. Older, larger females can produce five dozen or more young.

Adult females (and males, too) will eat any newborn guppies they can catch. Unless you take precautions in your aquarium, most of the newborn will be eaten. In the next chapter, we'll tell you what things you can do to prevent this from happening.

A day or two before the female gives birth she becomes very restless. She moves from one corner of the tank to another. She'll seek out a darkened spot under some plant leaves or in the shelter of a rock.

Most of the time birth takes place in the early morning, at least among the guppies we've kept. The female seems to quiver and tense her body. The vent begins to expand and the young are expelled in a head to tail position. Sometimes two or three are expelled almost in the same instant. In any case, births are usually very rapid.

The young fall through the water and their curled up bodies begin to stretch out. In just a few minutes they are swimming upward and into any available hiding places.

A newborn guppy seems to be mostly eyes and tail. Its body is almost transparent. Viewing a baby guppy from above with a magnifying lens you can see its swim bladder, brain, backbone and other organs through its skin.

Newborn guppies seem to be defenseless. Yet this tiny fish is well equipped to survive. It swims almost immediately after birth. Its jaw is fully developed so it can catch food. Its senses and nervous system are operating. From the moment of birth, a newborn guppy goes after food, flees from danger, and moves quickly and easily through the water.

(highly magnified)

male

female

young hiding in Nitella

Young guppies usually swim near the surface of the water. If you move your hand toward them, they will dive quickly to the bottom. If an adult fish or some other danger comes too near, the young guppies will streak off in different directions. If you provide them with enough hiding places, most of the young will escape being eaten.

If you provide them with plenty of food, newborn guppies will double their size in little more than one week. If you keep the young well fed, there is not much danger that they will eat one another. You can even keep several groups of young of different ages and sizes in the same aquarium.

A male guppy will reach full size in about twelve to fourteen weeks. His colors and gonopodium have developed even before that. A female takes several weeks longer than a male to become fully grown. Both males and females can breed before they are fully grown, but the young that are produced are usually smaller and less able to survive.

When a loaded female is moved to a new aquarium or if it is roughly handled, it may give birth prematurely. The premature young are not able to swim as well as fully developed newborn. They have a larger yolk sac, a food source which they used during development inside the mother's body. The yolk sac will help the premature young survive during the early days after birth.

Sometimes, but only rarely, a young guppy is born still within its egg membrane. The membrane is a thin, transparent covering in which the egg develops. Such young will die unless they can escape from the membrane.

double sword

lyretail

double sword

⋈ ⋈ ⋈ ⋈ ⋈ ⋈ ⋈ ⋈ ⋈ ⋈ ⋈ ⋈ ⋈ ⋈ ⋈ ⋈ ⋈ ⋈ ⋈

6.

breeding guppies

The problem with breeding guppies is not so much how to get them to breed but rather how to prevent them from breeding too soon and too often. Young guppies, raised with plenty of food and enough room in an aquarium, will be ready to breed in two months. If all you want are more guppy babies you have no problem. But, if you want to breed larger and showier guppies, two months is too soon to pick out the best fish to breed.

Outwardly, male and female guppies look the same at birth. In a few weeks the anal fin of the male begins to look more pointed. Colors may appear on the male. As soon as you notice these changes, remove the young males and place them in a separate aquarium.

Wait until the guppies are three or four months old before you allow them to breed. Select the largest and most attractive males for breeding. You can select males on the basis of their tail size or shape, color or color pattern, or any other traits that interest you. (See page

57 for a chart listing some of the guppy varieties that have been bred.)

Place two or three males in an aquarium along with the largest and best-looking females. You do not have to match the numbers of males and females exactly. Two or three males can mate with a large number of females.

Keep the temperature of the breeding tank between 75° and 80° F. (25° to 27° C.). Feed the fish with a varied diet three or four meals each day. Within two or three weeks start to check the bodies of the females. Look at them from the side or from above. The bodies of the loaded fish begin to bulge. The vent or the so called "gravid spot" begins to darken and enlarge.

With experience, you'll be able to tell by looking at the size and shape of the bulge about how long it will be before the female gives birth. Otherwise count on twenty-eight days after fertilization.

The fewer fishes present when the female gives birth, the better it will be both for the babies and for the mother. Of course, this also includes the males. They have fulfilled their function weeks before.

There are two ways that you can save the babies and prevent the

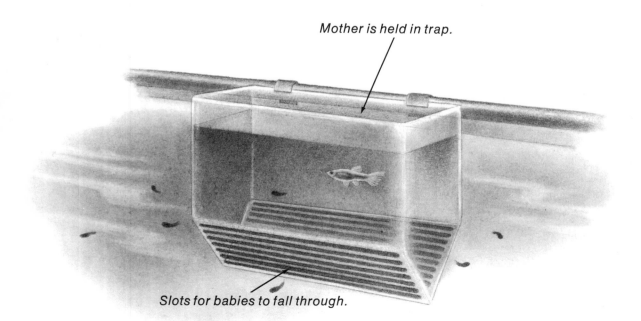

Mother is held in trap.

Slots for babies to fall through.

mother from eating them. One is to provide the breeding tank with plenty of extra plants for hiding spaces. Use a feathery leaf plant such as Myriophyllum or Cabomba. The other way is to use a device called a breeding trap.

Breeding traps are plastic cages that are hung on the side of the tank. They come in various shapes and sizes. The main idea in all of them is to keep the loaded female in a small space in which she can live for a few days. At the bottom of the cage are slots through which the newborn will fall or swim, and through which they cannot easily return.

Traps work fine for saving the young, but are not as good for the females. You must be gentle about placing them in the trap. Rough handling will result in injury or death. A day or two after the female gives birth she can be placed back in the aquarium.

Babies can be raised in the same tank with adults as long as there are plenty of hiding spaces among the plants. Of course, a separate tank that is used just for raising the young will insure that a larger number grow to maturity. But unless you have a special reason for wanting to raise lots of guppies, you might as well keep both the adults and the young in the same aquarium.

Remember that you must feed both the adults and the babies if you keep them in the same tank. The babies cannot eat food the size of adult food. If you use a flake food, crush some of it into a fine powder for the babies. You can purchase other kinds of foods that are made just for young fishes. During their first week, the newborn will eat tiny living things that are found in the water of most aquariums.

If you feed the babies two to four times each day and keep the aquarium at a temperature in the seventies, you'll be ready to breed them in three months. If you are not careful, you'll soon have guppies swimming in every available spare jar and dish in your house. As we said at the beginning of the chapter, the problem is not how to breed guppies but how to prevent them from overbreeding.

⋈ ⋈ ⋈ ⋈ ⋈ ⋈ ⋈ ⋈ ⋈ ⋈ ⋈ ⋈ ⋈ ⋈ ⋈ ⋈ ⋈ ⋈ ⋈

7.

what to do if your guppies become sick

In a large aquarium a guppy may become sick and die without you even being aware of it. Other guppies nibble at its body. In a few days the uneaten remains will rot. Before a week has gone by, the remains become part of the sediment that accumulates on the bottom of the tank.

Should you try to cure a sick guppy if you spot one? Probably not. It takes too much time and effort to cure one sick guppy, and the chances of success are not very great anyway. But in the case of a tankful of guppies all with the same sickness, you certainly should try to help.

Perhaps the most common cause of death on a large scale in an aquarium is some kind of poisoning. How can you tell if guppies are swimming in poisoned or polluted water? Here are a few ways that sick fish behave: Loss of appetite. Shimmying or shaking while remaining in one spot. Swimming on one side or upside down. Hanging close to the surface without moving. Lying on the bottom. Or, if several fish die suddenly, you may suspect something.

The poison that is responsible may be a mineral that is dissolved in the water such as copper. Copper or other minerals may be picked up by water that remains for long periods in the plumbing in your house. A preventive measure is to run the water from the tap for several minutes before using it in an aquarium. You should siphon out a gallon or two of water each week and replace it with fresh water. This will prevent a mineral build up.

Fresh water from a tap may kill guppies because of its chlorine content. Chlorine is put into water at water supply plants in order to kill germs and make the water safe to drink. You can clear chlorine from tap water by splashing the water as you pour it into a plastic pail. Then allow the water to age for twenty-four hours before you place it in the aquarium.

Another form of poisoning is carbon dioxide poisoning. This comes about because of overcrowding. Too much carbon dioxide is given off by the fish and there are not enough plants or light to use it for plant growth. You can spot this because the guppies will remain at the surface to try to get air. The solution is to prevent a tank from becoming overcrowded. Either transfer the excess fish to another tank or use an air pump to aerate the water.

Overfeeding can result in decaying food that pollutes and poisons the water. The poisons are produced by the bacteria growing in the food. The symptoms of fish suffering from food poisoning are similar to those of carbon dioxide poisoning. The solution is not to overfeed. For quick relief if the condition occurs, siphon out the decaying food along with several gallons of water and replace with fresh water.

Insect sprays, detergents, soaps, and aerosol sprays can also result in water poisoning. Some insect sprays are so deadly that even a trace as small as one drop in a twenty-gallon aquarium will kill all the fish.

The solution is to prevent all of these materials from coming into contact with the aquarium water. Don't spray in the same room as an aquarium. But if you must spray, cover the aquarium with a sheet of plastic and tape it tightly all the way around the edges. If you suspect that the water has been poisoned, quickly exchange large amounts with fresh water of the same temperature.

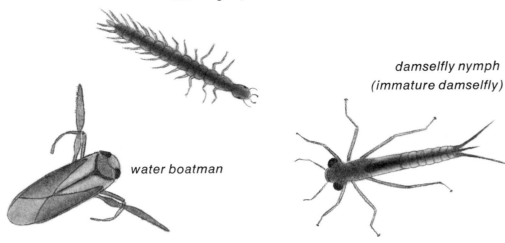

water tiger (larva of whirlgig beetle)

damselfly nymph
(immature damselfly)

water boatman

Insect enemies of guppies (magnified)

Other than poisoning, the most common illness of guppies is called Ich. The illness is caused by a tiny animal that lives on fishes. Ich is also called the white spot disease because that is just what it looks like. Sometimes a fish can be covered by white spots all over its fins and body. By that time it is probably too late to cure the illness and the fish will die.

Ich is very infectious, and all of the fish in your aquarium can come down with it unless they are treated. The treatment is to raise the water temperature to 85°F. (30°C.). Then add a chemical for the treatment of Ich which you can purchase at your local aquarium dealer. Be sure to follow the directions on the container exactly. Do not add more than is called for or you will kill your guppies.

After a period of ten days to make sure that all the Ich has been killed, lower the water temperature gradually over a period of several days. Replace a gallon of aquarium water with fresh water each day for a week or ten days. Check the fish carefully to see that no new white spots appear.

Sometimes a cottony or slimy white growth will appear on a guppy's body. This is probably some kind of fungus disease. A fungus is a kind of plant that grows on living or once-living material. Most commonly, guppies will suffer from mouth fungus.

You can try treating a guppy suffering from fungus by netting it from the aquarium and placing it into a solution made up of two table-spoonsful of ordinary non-iodized salt (such as kosher salt) and two tablespoonsful of Epsom salts in one gallon of water. The water solution should be at the same temperature as the aquarium water. Leave the fish in the solution for an hour before returning it to its aquarium. You may have to repeat the treatment for several days.

Most other kinds of illnesses are too difficult to treat. Some of these are fish tuberculosis (not contagious to humans), bloat, air bladder disease, and growths of various kinds. In most cases, if the fish does not get better by itself in a few days, it is best to put it to death painlessly.

Very rarely, you may accidentally introduce an insect or other animal enemy of a guppy into the tank. It may come into the aquarium along with daphnia or some other live foods that you use. Any insects swimming around your aquarium can be easily netted out before they cause much trouble.

mystery snail

pond snail

ramshorn snail

striped sucker catfish

⋈ ⋈ ⋈ ⋈ ⋈ ⋈ ⋈ ⋈ ⋈ ⋈ ⋈ ⋈ ⋈ ⋈ ⋈ ⋈ ⋈ ⋈

8.

what other animals can live with guppies?

Whether by accident or by purpose, snails seem to be present in most guppy tanks. Sooner or later a few tiny snails come in along with some plants. Or perhaps a plant leaf is carrying a little packet of snail's eggs in a jellylike coating. Whatever the reason, the snails will multiply their numbers quickly. Soon you'll be giving them away to your friends and anybody else who will take them.

Snails eat some of the leftover food that you feed the guppies. They will also eat algae growing on the sides of the aquarium or on the leaves of plants. But it takes an awful lot of snails to really keep algae from growing.

Snails have disadvantages, too. Guppies will often pick at the snails, bothering them. A lot of snails produce a lot of wastes. When snails die, their soft bodies rot in their shells. This also adds to the pollution in the tank. In fact, if one of the larger kinds of snails dies, the resulting pollution may kill some of the guppies. So if you decide to have snails, don't keep too many of them in your guppy tank. Some of the common kinds of snails that are sold by aquarium dealers are pond snails, Ram's Horn snails, and Mystery Snails.

Much better than snails in helping to clean up an aquarium of un-eaten food or algae are the many species of catfish. There are two main kinds. One kind are the bottom feeders. The other kind are the sucker cats. Both kinds are useful and will do well in a guppy aquarium.

Among the best of the bottom feeding kinds of catfish are the different species of *Corydoras*. These gentle fish with their downward pointing whiskers are industrious workers. They search continuously over the bottom of the tank for bits of leftover food. Larger and bulkier than guppies, *Corydoras* cats will never harm a guppy, not even a newborn one.

Two or three *Corydoras* cats in a ten-gallon tank will regularly turn over the gravel, nose in and among the plants, and keep any food that

saddle catfish
(Corydoras melanistius melanistius)

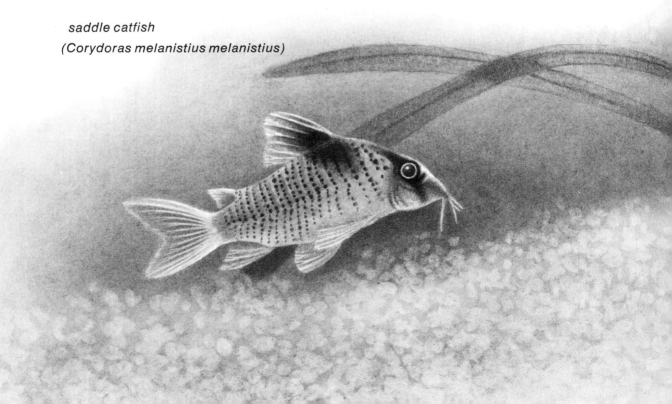

skunk catfish
(Corydoras arcuatus)

leopard catfish
(Corydoras leopardus)

black wag platies

male

female

female

swordtails

male

black mollies

male

female

falls on the bottom from rotting. In fact, it is a good idea to supply the cats with some extra food just so that they will not go hungry. Freeze-dried tubifex worms, available in most pet stores, make an excellent food for catfish.

Sucker cats will spend their time cleaning up any algae growing on the sides of the tank or on the leaves of plants. With sucker cats in your aquarium, you will never have to scrape off the algae growing on the front glass. Some of the more common species of sucker cats seen in aquariums are *Plecostomus, Otocinclus,* and *Loricaria. Otocinclus* cats are smaller than the other two kinds, but otherwise they all do the same kind of job.

Guppies will do well in an aquarium with other kinds of fishes as well as catfish. The important thing to remember is that guppies are small fish and they will be eaten by many other kinds of larger fishes. But there are many kinds of fishes that will not bother guppies at all.

Perhaps the best kinds of fishes to keep with guppies are some of the other common live-bearers such as platies, swordtails, and mollies. There are different species and varieties of each of these. Just as with guppies, fish breeders have developed differently colored and finned strains of the other live-bearers.

Platies are a bit larger and more full bodied than guppies. Some of the more popular varieties are the red or gold wagtail, the blue moon, the all-red or all-gold platy, and the spotted platy. Another kind of platy is called the *variatus*. It has mixed colors of gold with a red tail. All platies will interbreed with one another.

Platies get along at the same temperatures and water conditions as do guppies. They breed a bit more slowly but still very often. They like to pick at algae growing on plants or along the sides of the aquarium. Platies are a little less likely than guppies to eat their young.

The most popular kind of mollie is the black mollie. Its body is jet black and looks like velvet. Other kinds of mollies are spotted black, red, or blue. Adult mollies are larger than guppies but will not bother the adults, though they will eat the babies.

Mollies are more difficult to keep than guppies or platies. They need a slightly higher temperature than guppies, about 78° F. (26° C.). They also do better with a small amount of salt added to the water in their aquarium, about one teaspoonful to every five gallons.

Mollies need a lot of algae or other vegetable matter in their diets. If there is not enough algae growing in the tank, add a few small pieces of lettuce or a little chopped boiled spinach each day. Mollies should be fed at least three or four small meals a day. At the end of the day remove any uneaten bits of lettuce or spinach.

Any rough handling will usually result in the female mollie giving birth prematurely. The best thing to do is never to move a loaded female mollie from one tank to another. Baby mollies are much larger than baby guppies or baby platies. Provide them with plenty of hiding places if you want any to survive.

Swordtails are the largest of the common live-bearers. An adult swordtail male is about three inches long, not including its sword. The sword itself may be almost as long as the rest of the body. Swordtails have been bred in different colors much the same as platies.

Swordtails eat algae and other plant materials. You can feed them in the same way that you feed mollies. Swordtails do not do well in cooler waters. Keep them at about the same temperature as mollies.

Swordtails need more room than the other live-bearers. At least a fifteen-gallon tank is necessary for them to grow to full size. A large female is able to give birth to one hundred to two hundred young. You can see that you'll need plenty of aquarium space if you decide to breed swordtails.

There are many kinds of fishes other than live-bearers that can be kept with guppies. Besides keeping fishes that are about the same size, it's a good idea to choose fishes that have the same water and temperature requirements, or do some research in one of the books listed on page 61.

finding out more
about guppies

You may think of other questions about guppies. Does a guppy sleep during the night? Do young guppies swim together in schools? Do guppies keep growing all of their lives or do they reach a certain size and remain there? Do guppies do better in tanks that are lighted all day and all night?

Nobody can answer every question that you may think of about guppies. But you may be able to find the answer to some of these questions yourself. Observe your guppies each day. Keep notes on what you see so that you don't forget. You can make drawings or take photos to help you remember.

Perhaps you can do an experiment to help you find out the answer to a question. In an experiment, you will want to set up at least two groups so that you can compare what happens. Each group should be set up with the same number of guppies and with the same conditions except for the one factor that you are testing.

For example, suppose you are trying to find out whether guppies do better with one kind of food or another. You would set up the same number of the same age guppies in two different aquariums. Both aquariums should be the same size and lighted in the same way. The only difference would be in the way you feed the guppies in each tank.

Some experiments might take you several weeks or longer. Others might take only a few days. With any experiment you will have to think about your results to see what conclusion you could come to. Perhaps a friend can do the same experiment to see whether you both get the same results. Any conclusion you come to should be checked to make sure that it is correct.

The guppies in your aquarium are living creatures that you have decided to care for. You have certain responsibilities for their care. They are no longer able to care for themselves as they would in nature. You are the one who must feed and maintain them.

Any experiments that you do with guppies should be to find out about their normal activities, breeding, and behavior. None of your studies should result in guppies suffering pain or unnecessary discomfort. If you begin to neglect the care of your guppies, then it may be time to give away your guppies to a friend who is interested in caring for them.

Guppies are wonderful pets to keep around the house. They demand little space and effort on your part. And they will reward you with a fascinating glimpse of the world of nature whenever you care to look.

delta tail

veiltail

swordtail

some types of guppies

1. Delta Tail

The caudal fin is approximately an equilateral (all its sides are equal) triangle. The dorsal fin is approximately a parallelogram (a four-sided figure whose opposite sides are parallel). Both fins are entirely colored along with color on at least half the body.

2. Veiltail

The body and the caudal fin are approximately even in length. The caudal fin is approximately an isosceles (two equal sides) triangle. Both fins are entirely colored along with color on at least half the body.

3. Swordtail

The dorsal fin shall be long and narrow. The upper part of the caudal fin is also long and swordlike. The dorsal fin is colored. The caudal fin may be clear or colored.

4.

Other types are less common than those listed above. The names usually describe their appearance.
   a. Roundtail: Caudal fin evenly rounded.
   b. Double Sword: Caudal fin has a top and bottom swordlike projection.
   c. Lyretail: Like a double sword but not curved and not so long.
   d. Speartail: Broad caudal fin tapers to a point.

5.

Color varieties occur in many different shades. The most common are blue, black, red, green, and multicolor. These are the colors of the male's caudal fins and usually the dorsals. The background colors of the body are usually gray, gold, or albino with many variations.

Note: These descriptions have taken into account standards set up by the American Guppy Association and the British Guppy Breeders Society.

roundtail

double sword

lyretail

speartail

⋈ ⋈ ⋈ ⋈ ⋈ ⋈ ⋈ ⋈ ⋈ ⋈ ⋈ ⋈ ⋈ ⋈ ⋈ ⋈ ⋈ ⋈

books and magazines
for reading and research

BOOKS

Atz, James. *Aquarium Fishes: Their Beauty, History, and Care.* New York: Viking, 1971.

Axelrod, Herbert. *Tropical Fish as a Hobby.* New York: McGraw, 1969.

Cust, George and Bird, Peter. *Tropical Freshwater Aquaria.* New York: Bantam, 1972.

Innes, William. *Exotic Aquarium Fishes.* New York: Dutton, 19th Edition.

Julian, T. W. *The Dell Encyclopedia of Tropical Fish.* New York: Delacorte.

Madsen, J. M. *Aquarium Fishes in Color.* New York: Macmillan, 1975.

Schiotz, Arne. *A Guide to Aquarium Fishes and Plants.* New York: Lippincott, 1972.

Thorn, John and Thorn, Jose. *Starting with Tropical Fish.* New York: Scribner, 1974.

Wainright, Neil. *Tropical Aquariums, Plants, and Fishes.* New York: Warne, 1970.

MAGAZINES

Tropical Fish Hobbyist Magazine, P. O. Box 27, Neptune, N.J. 07753

Aquarium Digest International, c/o Tetra Sales (USA), 21393 Curtis Street, Hayward, Ca. 94545

index

a

air bladder (swim bladder), 24, 31
    disease of, 43
air pumps, 13, 17, 40
algae, 10–11, 17, 45, 50
American Guppy Association, 56
animals compatible with guppies,
    45–51
appearance, 21–25
appetite, loss of, 39
aquariums, 2, 4–5
    cleaning of, 8, 17
    gravel for, 9–10
    maintenance of, 7–13
    plants for, 9

    sediment in, 10, 39, 45
    separate tanks, need for, 35,
      37
    size of, 25, 51

b

babies. *See* newborn
backbone, 31
birth, 5, 30, 36
bloat, 43
blood vessels, 25–27
bottom feeding cats, 46
brain, 31
breeding, 4–5, 33, 35–37
breeding trap, 37